History *of* Britain

Henry VIII

Andrew Langley

Illustrated by John James

HAMLYN

HISTORY OF BRITAIN – HENRY VIII
was produced for Hamlyn Children's Books
by Lionheart Books, London

Editor: Lionel Bender
Designer: Ben White
Editorial Assistant: Madeleine Samuel
Picture Researcher: Jennie Karrach
Media Conversion and Typesetting:
  Peter MacDonald

Educational Consultant: Jane Shuter
Editorial Advisors: Andrew Farrow, Paul Shuter

Production Controller: Christine Campbell
Editorial Director: David Riley

First published in Great Britain in 1995
by Hamlyn Children's Books,
an imprint of Reed International Books,
Michelin House, 81 Fulham Road, London SW3 6RB,
and Auckland, Melbourne, Singapore and Toronto.

Copyright © 1995 Reed International Books Limited

ISBN 0 600 58614 6 Hb
ISBN 0 600 58621 9 Pb

British Library Cataloguing-in-Publication Data.
A catalogue record for this book is available
from the British Library.

Printed and bound in China

Acknowledgements
All illustrations by John James except maps, by Hayward Art
Group.
Picture credits
BAL = The Bridgeman Art Library, London., NPG = By courtesy
of the National Portrait Gallery, London, MC = The Mansell
Collection,
RC = The Royal Collection Enterprises Limited/© 1995 Her
Majesty the Queen. MEPL = Mary Evans Photo Library.
l = left, r = right, t = top, b = bottom, c = centre.
Pages: 4: Weidenfeld and Nicolson Archive/Bibliotheque Méjanes,
Aix-en-Provence. 5t: BAL/Kunsthistorisches Museum, Vienna. 5c:
© Royal College of Arms. 5bl: Ashmolean Museum, Oxford. 6l:
BAL/Louvre, Paris. 6-7b: MEPL. 7tl: NPG. 7br: © Royal
Armouries, Tower of London. 8t: e.t.archive. 8b: RC. 9t:
BAL/Fitzwilliam Museum, University of Cambridge. 9b: BAL/British
Library, London. 10bl: © Oeffentliche Kunstsammlung, Basel.
Inv.1662.31, Kat. 1988 Nr.65. 10tr: Weidenfeld and Nicolson
Archive. 10cr: Michael Holford. 11: NPG. 12: Jean Williamson/
Mick Sharp. 13t: NPG. 13b: MC. 14tl: National Gallery of Art,
Washington/Andrew W. Mellon Collection. 1937.1.64 (PA) 64.
14bl: © Royal College of Arms. 14tr: NPG. 15tl: RC. 16: NPG.
17t: © British Library/Cotton Augustus I. i. 22/23. 17cr: The
Slide File, Dublin. 17bl: BAL/British Library, London. 18:
BAL/Giraudon/Louvre, Paris. 19t: With Permission of the Fellows
and Trustees of King's College, Cambridge. 19cr: BAL/British
Museum, London. 19bl: NPG. 20cl: Staatliche Graphische
Sammlung, Munchen. Inv. Nr. 12875. 19bc: Society of
Antiquities, London. 20-21t: © Mary Rose Trust. 21: Portsmouth
City Council. 22bl: National Museum of Wales. 22tr: Aerofilms.
22br: Public Record Office, London/Geremy Butler Photography.
Cover: Photos: (Henry VIII in a bedroom, reading) BAL/British
Library, London, (Henry trampling the Pope) MC, (Henry VIII's
glove) Ashmolean Museum, Oxford, (detail of Henry with Edward
and Jane Seymour) RC.

PLACES TO VISIT

Here are some sites associated with the life and times of
Henry VIII. Your local Tourist Office will be able to tell you
about other places in your area.

Castle Acre Priory, Norfolk. Ruins of a dissolved priory.
Compton Wynyates, Warwickshire. A splendid Tudor house,
dedicated to King Henry.
Deal Castle, Kent. Good example of the defences built in
Henry's reign.
Hampton Court Palace, London. Built by Wolsey, then taken
over by Henry. Has a famous maze.
Hever Castle, Kent. Moated home of Anne Boleyn's family.
Henry wooed her here.
Holyrood Palace, Edinburgh. Splendid royal house, convert-
ed from an abbey by King James V.
Mary Rose, Portsmouth. The flagship of Henry's navy, pre-
served and on display, with many weapons and other objects
of the time.
National Portrait Gallery, London. Many paintings of major
Tudor personalities.
Ormondes Castle, Tipperary, Eire. Tudor manor house,
thought to be the birthplace of Anne Boleyn.
Rievaulx Abbey, Yorkshire. Ruins of a dissolved abbey.
Tintern Abbey, Gwent. Ruined abbey in dramatic setting.
Tower of London Site of imprisonments and executions, with
a fine collection of weapons and armour.
Yarmouth Castle, Isle of Wight. Good example of the
defences built in Henry's reign.

INTRODUCTION

Henry VIII was the most famous of the Tudor kings. Yet he should never have been king at all. Born on 28 June 1491, he was only the second son of Henry VII. His elder brother, Arthur, was set to become the next ruler.

At this time, there was great danger of rebellion or civil war. Henry VII had brought peace to England by uniting the rival families of Lancaster and York in 1485. But he still had many enemies among the nobles. It was vital that he should have a strong and capable son to take the throne after him.

In 1501, Arthur married a Spanish princess, Catherine of Aragon. But only a few months later he died of disease. At the age of 10, Henry was heir, or successor, to the English throne.

CONTENTS

THE YOUNG KING   4

Henry VIII's seal

WAR AND PEACE   6

The Tudor Rose

LIFE AT COURT   8

Gold emblem of Pope Clement VII

ANNE BOLEYN   10

Henry VIII's writing box

THE BREAK WITH ROME   12

The ruins of a dissolved priory

BIRTH OF AN HEIR   14

Henry's bedchamber door lock

BLOOD AND REBELLION   16

Henry VIII's armour

THE LAST THREE QUEENS   18

White Tower at the Tower of London

OLD HARRY   20

Henry VIII's astrolabe

DEATH OF THE KING   22

Henry VIII's personal rings

GLOSSARY – DEFINITIONS OF IMPORTANT WORDS   23

TIMECHART   23

INDEX   24

THE YOUNG KING

Henry was crowned king on 24 June 1509. The scholar Thomas More wrote: "This day is the end of our slavery, the fount of our liberty; the end of sadness, the beginning of joy." Like many other people, More believed that Henry VIII would be a more generous ruler than Henry VII had been.

The new king certainly looked like a hero. He was tall and handsome, with bright eyes and red hair. Strong and full of energy, he loved to spend hours playing tennis or hunting. Sometimes he would tire out eight horses in a single day, riding one after the other. He was also highly skilled with sword and spear, and took part in many mock fights called jousts.

But Henry was a scholar as well as a sportsman. He spoke French, Latin and Spanish. He sang well, wrote music, and played the lute and harpsichord. He was deeply interested in religious writings, as well as mathematics and astronomy.

▷ **A drawing of the future Henry VIII as a young child.**

▷ **King Henry on horseback in a royal forest** (far right), hawking with his courtiers and servants. The hunters carry the hawks on their arms, and release them to fly after rabbits and partridges. In front of the king is Charles Brandon, his favourite companion. Brandon later married Henry's sister, Mary.

Henry made himself even more popular by getting rid of many of his father's old advisors. Among these were Richard Empson and Edmund Dudley, two hated collectors of taxes. Both were executed in 1510.

However, the young king was often too busy to attend to the running of the country. He was encouraged to enjoy himself by his noblemen, who wanted to regain their power. The king was kept busy with banquets and hunting. The grandest celebrations of all followed Henry's marriage to Catherine of Aragon and, early in 1511, when the queen gave birth to a son. But the little prince died only two months later.

△ **The young Catherine of Aragon.** She was only 16 when Arthur died. Her marriage had been part of a treaty between England and Spain, which were both Roman Catholic countries. It was now agreed that Catherine should marry Henry. But the Church forbade men from marrying their brother's widow. Special permission was given by the Pope, and the marriage took place in 1509.

◁ **Henry's hawking glove,** decorated with jewels. It was worn to protect his arm from the hawk's sharp talons when he carried the bird out hunting.

△ **Henry at a joust** in 1511, held to celebrate the birth of his son. Catherine watches from the stand. The horse's covers are embroidered with threads of pure gold.

WAR AND PEACE

Fighting at jousts was not enough for Henry. He wanted the glory of a real war. Above all, he wanted a war against France. Like some English kings before him, Henry claimed to be the rightful ruler of France.

Henry made an agreement with Spain and the Holy Roman Empire to act against France. In June 1513, Henry and his troops landed at Calais on the French coast. They set out to conquer territory. The towns of Therouanne and Tournai quickly surrendered, and the English won a minor battle. But there was trouble at home. The Scottish king, James IV, invaded northern England in support of France. An English army defeated him at Flodden after a fierce battle. More than 10,000 Scots were killed, including James himself.

△ **Francis I**, who became king of France in 1515. Henry, with his army, met Francis and his troops at the Field of the Cloth of Gold (right). They swore friendship, but were at war again within two years.

▷ **English troops charge the Scots** at the Battle of Flodden. At this time, Scotland was an independent country. The Scottish king, James IV, had married Henry's sister, Margaret, but still supported France against the Tudor monarchs.

CARDINAL WOLSEY

△ **Thomas Wolsey**, a butcher's son who became the most powerful man in England after the king. Ambitious and greedy, he also became very wealthy. By 1520, he was not only Lord Chancellor, but leader of the King's Council, an Archbishop and special ambassador for the Pope.

Henry felt that his first war in France had been a triumph. He planned a fresh expedition to France for the following year. But the fighting had wasted a lot of money and men, and gained little land.

The king now had a new advisor, Thomas Wolsey. Wolsey saw that more war was useless, and persuaded Henry to make peace with France in August 1514. The French allowed him to keep Tournai, and gave Henry much gold.

Wolsey grew more powerful, and became Lord Chancellor of England in 1515. Henry was bored by the daily work of government, so Wolsey did it for him. Wolsey's greatest achievement was to prevent war with France for eight years. In 1520 he organized a meeting at Calais between Henry and Francis, the French king. Richly decorated tents were put up for the occasion so the place was called The Field of the Cloth of Gold.

▷ **A suit of armour** made for Henry VIII. It can be seen today in the Tower of London.

LIFE AT COURT

For the first half of his reign, Henry spent much time enjoying himself. In the summer, he went on long hunting expeditions, staying at one of his many palaces. During the winter, he remained near London. Wherever he went, he was attended by the members of his court, and by an army of servants.

The most important part of any palace was the Privy Chamber. This was the king's private apartment, where he slept and ate. Even here, he was surrounded by 80 of his closest courtiers, as well as doctors, messengers and musicians.

Other parts of each royal palace were also huge. The kitchens and wine cellars alone needed more than 350 staff. Among the hundreds of other servants were rat-catchers, pages, gardeners and stable lads. They were all under the command of the Lord Steward.

Henry's court lived in a very grand way. In 1517, for example, the king and queen held a banquet for ambassadors from Spain. The meal itself lasted for seven hours. The English courtiers were richly dressed, but Henry's costume was most magnificent of all. He wore a white, embroidered robe decorated with roses made from rubies and diamonds.

This luxury used up a vast amount of money. So did Henry's wars with France. One expedition alone cost over £500,000. As a result, the king quickly wasted the wealth carefully built up by his father, Henry VII. He was forced to ask Parliament to raise money from extra taxes. This made him unpopular both with nobles and ordinary people.

▷ **Gold half sovereign coin of Henry VIII.**

△ **The king in the House of Lords attending Parliament in 1523.** The judges sit in the centre on woolsacks. The bishops are on the left and the nobles on the right. The members of the House of Commons stand in a group to the right of the king.

◁ **A Dutch painting of Henry VIII at the age of 35.**

▽ **Henry VIII dining alone** in his Privy Chamber. The servants bringing food and drink kneel in front of him, while musicians play a fanfare. Courtiers stand beside Henry.

▽ **Henry playing the harp**, from an illustration in the king's own book of psalms. Beside Henry stands Will Somers, a servant whose job was to amuse the king.

ANNE BOLEYN

By the mid-1520s, Catherine had borne four sons, but all of them had died. Only one daughter, Mary, survived. Catherine was now nearly too old to have any more children. The king desperately wanted a son to succeed him. Without a male heir, the reign of Tudor monarchs was in danger of ending.

Henry began to think that God was punishing him and Catherine. They should never have been married at all, because Catherine was his dead brother's wife. The Pope ought not to have allowed the wedding.

Then, early in 1526, Henry met a new lady of the court, Anne Boleyn. He fell in love with her immediately. Though Henry normally hated writing, he sent Anne a stream of love letters, begging her to be his mistress. Anne refused. She told Henry that he must make her his wife. Leaving the court, she went to her father's castle at Hever in Kent.

△ **One of Henry's love letters to Anne Boleyn**, written in 1528. His signature HR (R for the Latin *rex*, king) can be seen at the bottom.

▷ **The king meets with Anne** at Hever Castle.

△ **Hampton Court Palace**, built for Wolsey but given to Henry in 1529.

◁ **Thomas More** (centre) and his family, sketched by Hans Holbein. The artist has scribbled each person's name on their costumes. More became Lord Chancellor after Wolsey in 1529.

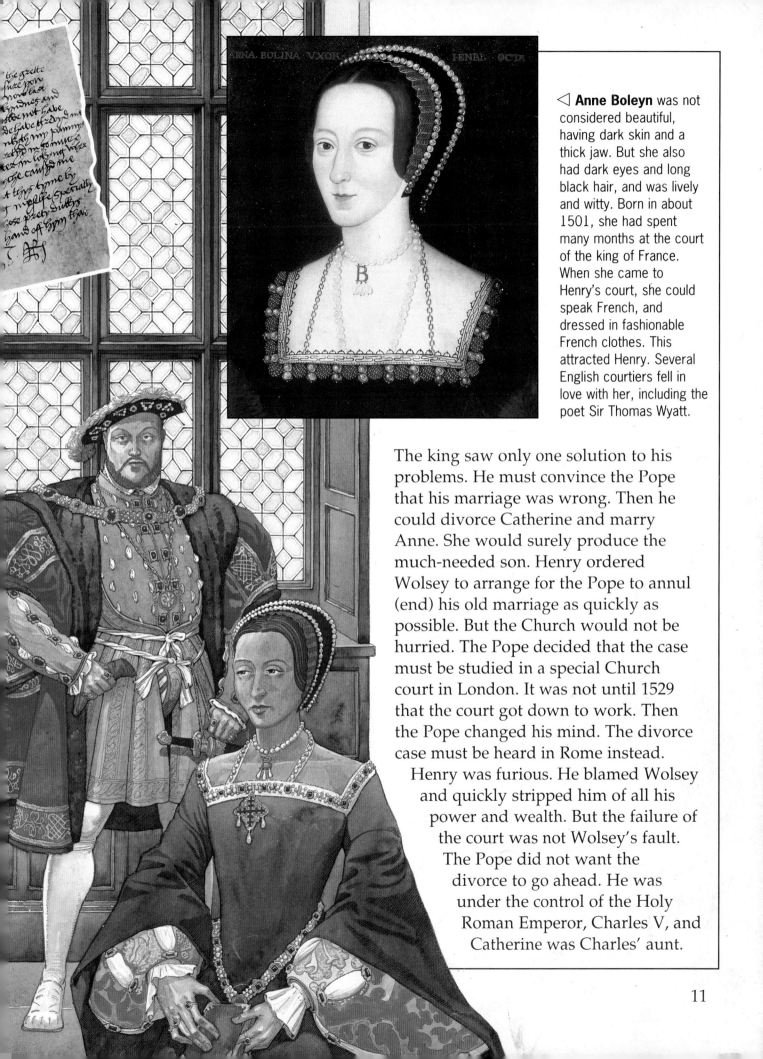

ANNA BOLINA VXOR HENRI OCTA

◁ **Anne Boleyn** was not considered beautiful, having dark skin and a thick jaw. But she also had dark eyes and long black hair, and was lively and witty. Born in about 1501, she had spent many months at the court of the king of France. When she came to Henry's court, she could speak French, and dressed in fashionable French clothes. This attracted Henry. Several English courtiers fell in love with her, including the poet Sir Thomas Wyatt.

The king saw only one solution to his problems. He must convince the Pope that his marriage was wrong. Then he could divorce Catherine and marry Anne. She would surely produce the much-needed son. Henry ordered Wolsey to arrange for the Pope to annul (end) his old marriage as quickly as possible. But the Church would not be hurried. The Pope decided that the case must be studied in a special Church court in London. It was not until 1529 that the court got down to work. Then the Pope changed his mind. The divorce case must be heard in Rome instead.

Henry was furious. He blamed Wolsey and quickly stripped him of all his power and wealth. But the failure of the court was not Wolsey's fault. The Pope did not want the divorce to go ahead. He was under the control of the Holy Roman Emperor, Charles V, and Catherine was Charles' aunt.

11

THE BREAK WITH ROME

The king was determined to marry Anne Boleyn. But he refused to go to Rome to hear the divorce case. That would make him seem weak and humble. Instead, he turned to Parliament for help. Henry knew that many Members of Parliament disliked the power of the Roman Catholic Church.

Henry himself was a loyal Catholic. Early in his reign, the German Martin Luther had protested at the way the Catholic Church was run. Henry had written a book attacking Luther. For this, the Pope had given Henry the title "Defender of the Faith" in 1521. However, Catholicism was deeply unpopular in England. Many priests were greedy and ignorant. They drank too much and did little work. Ordinary people hated the Church's huge wealth (it owned about one-third of all land). Worse still, they hated having to pay taxes such as tithes (a part of their earnings) to the local priest.

▷ **Dissolution of the Monasteries.** In 1536 and 1539, Parliament passed Acts 'dissolving', or getting rid of, religious houses. Monks and nuns were sent away, their treasures given to the king, and the buildings plundered. The ruins of Tintern Abbey, dissolved in 1536, remain today (above right).

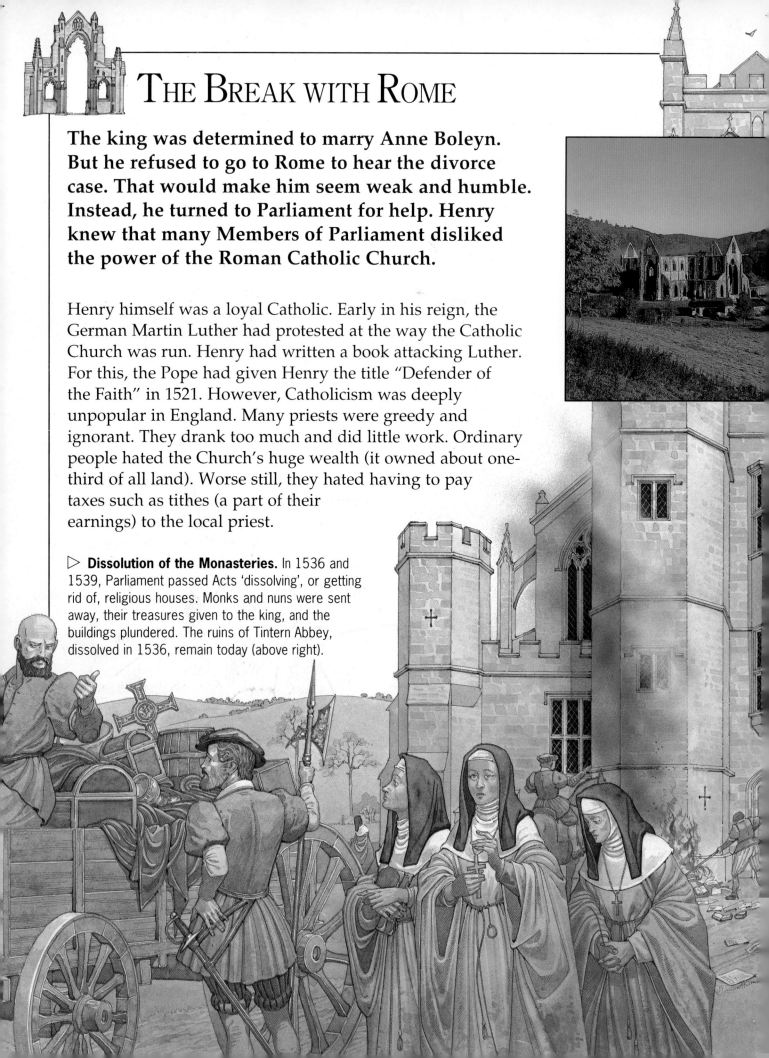

EARL OF ESSEX.

△ **Thomas Cromwell** was the king's chief minister from 1533 to 1540. This portrait was by the court painter Hans Holbein. Cromwell was clever and hard-working, and not interested in riches.

Henry struck his first blow against the Church in 1530. Parliament accused priests of being more loyal to the Pope than to the king. In 1532, Henry demanded that priests swear loyalty to him as "Supreme Head of the English Church". The Lord Chancellor, Thomas More, refused to agree to this and resigned. In his place, Henry appointed Thomas Cromwell. After this, events happened very fast. Anne became pregnant with Henry's child in January 1533. She and the king were secretly married. The new Archbishop of Canterbury, Thomas Cranmer, gave Henry his divorce. By June 1533, Anne had been crowned as queen.

Henry had ignored the Pope in all this. Next, he and Cromwell encouraged Parliament to pass a series of laws which broke all links with Rome. One law stopped the payment of taxes to the Pope. Another law made the children of Anne and Henry heirs to the throne.

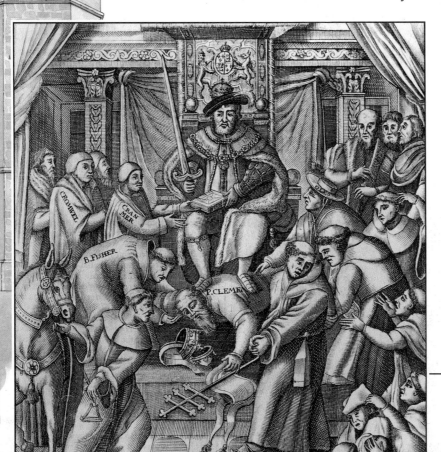

◁ **Henry trampling the Pope.** This imaginary scene shows Henry – sitting on the throne of England – trampling the Pope, Clement VII, underfoot. Henry is being helped by Cromwell and Cranmer (standing on the left) as Members of Parliament (on the right) and Roman Catholic priests (in the foreground) look on. In 1534 Parliament passed the Act of Supremacy, giving Henry complete control of the English Church.

BIRTH OF AN HEIR

Henry's first two wives died during 1536. In January, Catherine died, lonely and wretched. Anne Boleyn was beheaded in May. Her only child was a girl, Elizabeth. Anne had been found guilty of adultery. This was treason, and the punishment was death.

▷ **Portrait of Henry VIII painted in 1536**, the year of his marriage to Jane Seymour.

△ **Prince Edward** at the age of two. The picture was a gift from Hans Holbein to the king.

▽ **Queen Jane's coat-of-arms** and motto, or saying, "Bound to Obey and Serve".

Only a few days after Anne's execution, Henry was married again. His new wife was the quiet and modest Jane Seymour. The need for a son was now even more urgent. The king was 45 years old, and growing fatter and less healthy. At any moment he might catch the deadly 'sweating sickness' that was sweeping the country.

Soon after his wedding, Henry forced a new law through Parliament. It barred the baby Princess Elizabeth from ever becoming ruler of England. Catherine's daughter, Mary, had already been prevented from being monarch. Now only Jane's children could succeed him.

Jane brought happiness to the royal household. Princess Mary was brought back to court after a childhood in exile. Better still, in October 1537, Jane gave birth to a son, Edward. The king was overjoyed, and the whole country celebrated. But the joy was soon spoiled. Only 12 days after Edward's birth, the queen died of fever and infection. Henry's third marriage had lasted less than two years.

After his christening, Edward was proclaimed Prince of Wales. It was a sign of the new union, or link, between England and Wales, which had been made law in 1536. The union allowed England to rule over Wales. Many Welsh customs were abolished.

△ (Top) **Henry VIII sits with his arm round the shoulder of his son, Edward.** On the king's left is Jane Seymour. The picture cannot have been painted from life because Jane died shortly after she had Edward. It is part of a much bigger painting that also shows the two princesses, Mary on one side and Elizabeth on the other. Thus, all of Henry's surviving children appear together. They each ruled in turn. Edward reigned from 1547 to 1553, Mary from 1553 to 1558, and Elizabeth from 1558 to 1603.

△ **The grand christening of Prince Edward** in the chapel at Hampton Court Palace in 1537. Trumpeters played and attendants with fire torches lit the way as the baby was carried in by noblemen behind archbishops, bishops and chapel boys (shown here). Edward's sister, Mary, acted as godmother.

15

Blood and Rebellion

"I die loyal to God and the King, but to God first of all." These were the final words of Sir Thomas More before he was beheaded in 1535. He was sentenced to death for refusing to recognize that Henry was the Supreme Head of the English Church. More insisted that the Pope was the Church's leader.

More was one of the first people to be executed for not agreeing with Henry's new religious laws. Another was John Fisher, Bishop of Rochester. In the same year, three monks were hanged and then cut up while still alive. Several more were tortured and put to death. In 1534, Lord Offaly led a revolt against English power in Ireland. Henry ordered his troops to crush the rebels with great brutality.

▷ **Thomas Cranmer**, who was Archbishop of Canterbury from 1532 to 1556. He believed in the absolute power of the king, and helped to arrange Henry's marriages and divorces. With Cromwell, Cranmer encouraged the use of the Bible in English, which helped establish the Protestant Church in England.

▷ (Far right) **Sir Thomas More**, imprisoned in the Tower of London, watches as monks are dragged away on hurdles to be hanged. More was kept in the Tower for a year before he was beheaded.

△ **The sea defences at Dover.** By 1538, the Pope had called on other European monarchs to attack Henry for the break with Rome. Henry built new castles, for example Dublin's (right), with a tower and church, to defend his lands.

△ **Henry at prayer** in his private room at Windsor Castle. He never gave up the Catholic faith, despite his dislike for the Pope. He made a constant study of religion, and often went to Mass three times a day.

Henry's actions were very unpopular, especially in the north of England. Many people had relied on the monasteries for work or charity, and were angry when they closed. Others were alarmed at the threat of new taxes, and the spread of new 'Protestant' (non-Catholic) ideas.

The first uprising against Henry took place in Lincolnshire in October 1536. Riots soon spread across the country to Yorkshire and Cumbria. Here the leader was Robert Aske. He organized a peaceful 'Pilgrimage of Grace' to protest at the closing down of monasteries. Henry promised to pardon the rebels if they went home quietly. But when another riot broke out in 1537, his forces crushed the rebels savagely. More than 70 rebels and 'pilgrims' were hanged in Cumbria alone.

THE LAST THREE QUEENS

Henry had a son at last. But his defiance of the Pope had made him many enemies in Europe. Henry's best way of finding an ally was to marry the daughter of a European prince. In 1538, Cromwell began his search for a new wife for the king.

▷ **Anne of Cleves**, painted by Holbein. Cromwell's agents in Germany reported that she was good-looking and very talented. In fact, she was plain, shy and clumsy. Worse still, she knew nothing about music (one of Henry's loves) and could not speak English. But she came to like England. After the divorce, she lived in a house given her by the king. Henry treated her as a friend. Anne died in 1557.

It was not easy. Several princesses and duchesses were suggested. Then court artist Hans Holbein was sent to paint their portraits. These were shown to Henry. He found some of the women very attractive, but no marriages could be arranged.

In March 1539, Cromwell told Henry about a beautiful German princess, Anne of Cleves. The king eagerly agreed to marry her. When Anne arrived in England, he rushed to see her. To his horror, he found that she was far from beautiful. She was also Protestant. Their marriage was a disaster. Before the end of 1540, Henry and Anne were divorced.

Henry blamed Cromwell for misleading him. Cromwell was arrested and accused of trying to make England a Protestant country. He was found guilty of treason and beheaded in June 1540.

Henry gave up the idea of making an alliance by marriage in Europe. Soon after divorcing Anne, he married a pretty maid of honour at court called Catherine Howard. She was 20 years old.

△ **A stained glass painting of Catherine Howard.** Henry cried when he heard that she was unfaithful.

◁ **Catherine Howard** kneels to lay her head on the block at the Tower of London before her execution in February 1542.

◁ **Catherine Parr**, the sixth and final wife of Henry VIII. She lived until 1548.

△ **Nonsuch**, Henry's palace in Surrey begun in 1538. It was used as a palace by his children too.

KATHARINE PARRE

Once again, Henry had made a bad choice. Catherine flirted with the king's courtiers, and took several lovers. When the king found out, he felt humiliated. In his rage, he ordered that the queen and her lovers should be arrested. Catherine was beheaded early in 1542.

Henry married his last wife, Catherine Parr, in July 1543. She was a quiet and sensible woman, who looked after the king as he grew more ill. And she was a loving mother to his three children.

OLD HARRY

The king was 50 years old in 1541. He could barely walk, and sores on his legs were sometimes so painful that he could hardly speak either. He was fatter than ever. Yet he wanted one last triumph. He decided to lead an army to France once again.

▷ **Items from the wreck** of Henry's flagship, *Mary Rose*, which sank in 1545. The ship was raised from the seabed in 1971.

First, Henry had to make sure that the Scots would not attack him from the north. The Scottish king, James V, was Henry's nephew. But he still supported the French and refused to sign a peace treaty with England. In 1542, Henry's army beat the Scots at Solway Moss. James died soon after. His baby daughter, Mary, became ruler of Scotland.

By 1543, Henry had worked out a new treaty with the Scots. His son, Prince Edward, would marry Queen Mary. But the Scots rejected the treaty. Angrily, Henry sent an army to punish them. English troops attacked Leith and Edinburgh, causing great damage.

△ **Henry VIII in old age**, drawn by Holbein. Since the fall of Cromwell, Henry had governed by himself. Already ruler of England and Wales, he wanted to extend his power to the rest of Britain. In 1541 he was named king of Ireland. In 1542 he tried to overcome Scotland.

◁ **Henry's soldiers set up their camp** at the start of the siege of Boulogne in 1544. This picture shows the king's own tents at the bottom. In the centre men are bringing in horses and cannons, and setting up tents in the rain. At the top left, Boulogne is shown burning.

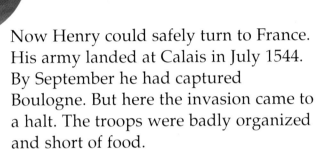

Now Henry could safely turn to France. His army landed at Calais in July 1544. By September he had captured Boulogne. But here the invasion came to a halt. The troops were badly organized and short of food.

Worse news came early in 1545. The Scots had taken revenge for the attacks on their towns, and defeated an English army at Ancrum Moor. That summer, a French fleet set sail to raid ports on the south coast of England. Henry was threatened on two sides. But he had built up a powerful English navy, with over 50 warships. This was easily able to keep control of the English Channel.

Henry at last made peace with France in June 1546. His campaign had been a waste of time and lives. It had also used up much of the wealth seized during the closure of the monasteries.

▷ **Henry and his army** at Portsmouth in July 1545. The king came to watch his navy gather in the harbour ready to meet the advancing French fleet. But strong winds and tides stopped the French from reaching the coast, though they landed on the Isle of Wight.

△ **The king watches in horror** as the *Mary Rose* sinks. The ship tilted in the wind, and water poured in through open gun ports. Over 500 men were drowned.

DEATH OF THE KING

"Of this I am sure, that charity was never so faint amongst you...nor God Himself was never less honoured and served." This is part of Henry's speech to his Parliament, made in 1545. He was sad that his break with Rome had caused so many arguments.

▽ **Deal Castle** in Kent, built by Henry in the late 1530s. It is in the shape of the Tudor rose.

It was the last time that the king spoke to the Lords and Commons. His health was now failing rapidly. Walking was agony for him, and he had to be hauled upstairs by a special crane. But his greatest worry was about who would rule after him. Prince Edward was only nine years old, and would need adults to help him govern.

In December 1546, as death drew nearer, Henry wrote his Will. He named his children, Edward, Mary and Elizabeth, to succeed him on the throne. He also appointed a council of 16 men to advise the prince until he was grown up. Weeks later, in January 1547, King Henry VIII died at the age of 55.

△ **An imaginary scene of Henry** with Mary (left), Edward (kneeling) and Elizabeth (right).

▷ **Henry VIII's Will**, or last wishes.

GLOSSARY

alliance an agreement to work or fight together.

ambassador an official who represents his country while living in another.

Catholic (Roman Catholic) a Christian who follows the religious leadership of the Pope in Rome.

civil war a war fought between groups of people in the same country.

court a king or queen's home and the people who live with and work for the monarch. Also a place where law trials are held.

government the people who run the country: the monarch, the Privy Council, Parliament and local government officials such as judges.

Lord Chancellor the monarch's chief advisor, who has charge of the courts of law.

monastery a place where monks live together, practising their religious beliefs.

nobles the rich and important men in the country, who had titles, such as Duke or Lord, and a lot of land.

Parliament the House of Lords (nobles and important churchmen) and the House of Commons (gentlemen elected by gentlemen)

meeting to advise the monarch. Only the monarch could summon, or call, Parliament.

Protestant a member of the Christian Church which separated from the Roman Catholic Church in the 16th century.

taxes money collected by the Church, nobles and the king to pay for buildings or to equip the army and navy.

tithe a tenth part of a person's income or produce. Tithes were taxes paid to support the clergy.

treaty an agreement between two countries or sides, for example, to end a war.

Henry VIII's Britain

This map shows the towns and cities mentioned in the book, including the Places to Visit listed on page 2.

including the Places to Visit listed on page 2.

Map of Henry VIII's Britain, showing: Leith, Edinburgh, Flodden Field, Ancrum Moor, Solway Moss, Rievaulx Abbey, Tipperary, Castle Acre Priory, Yarmouth Castle, Compton Wynyates, Tintern Abbey, Windsor, London, Nonsuch, Portsmouth, Dover, Calais, Hever Castle, Boulogne, Tournai, Deal, Isle of Wight.

TIMECHART

1491 Henry born
1501 Brother Arthur dies
1509 Henry becomes king. Marries Catherine of Aragon
1513 First expedition to invade France. Scots defeated at Flodden
1515 Wolsey becomes Lord Chancellor
1520 The Field of the Cloth of Gold
1521 Pope gives Henry the title of "Defender of the Faith"
1526 Henry falls in love with Anne Boleyn
1527 Henry attempts to divorce Catherine
1529 Fall of Wolsey
1531 Henry declares himself Supreme Head of the English church
1533 Henry gets his divorce from Catherine. He marries Anne Boleyn
1534 Act of Succession
1536 Dissolution of the monasteries begins. Union of England and Wales. Anne beheaded
1537 Birth of Edward. Death of Jane Seymour. Pilgrimage of Grace
1539 Larger monasteries closed down
1540 Henry marries and divorces Anne of Cleves
1542 Catherine Howard beheaded. Scots defeated at Solway Moss
1544 Henry's last attack on France
1547 Death of Henry

23

INDEX

Abbey
  Rievaulx 2
  Tintern 2, 14
Act of Supremacy 13, 23
Anne Boleyn 10, 11, 12, 13, 14, 23
Anne of Cleves 18, 19, 23
armour 7
Arthur (son of Henry VII) 3, 5, 23
Aske, Robert 17

banquets 5, 8
battles
  Ancrum Moor 21
  Boulogne 20
  Edinburgh 20
  Flodden 8
  Leith 20
  Solway Moss 20, 23
Boulogne 20, 21
Brandon, Charles 4

Calais 6, 7, 21
Canterbury, Archbishop of 13, 16
Catherine Howard 19, 23
Catherine of Aragon 3, 5, 10, 11, 14, 23
Catherine Parr 19
Charles V, Holy Roman Emperor 11
children (Henry's) 5, 10, 11, 13, 14, 15, 18
Church
  Catholic 5, 11, 12, 13, 23
  English 13, 16, 23
  Protestant 16
Clement VII 13
  see also Pope, the
clothes 5, 8, 11
coronation 4

court and courtiers 8, 9, 23
Cranmer, Archbishop Thomas 13, 16
Cromwell, Thomas 13, 16, 18, 19

Deal Castle 2, 22
death (of Henry VIII) 22, 23
Defender of the Faith 12, 23
divorce 11, 12, 13, 18, 23
Dublin Castle 17
Dudley, Edmund 5

education 4
Edward (son of Henry VIII & Jane Seymour) 14, 15, 20, 22, 23
Elizabeth, (daughter of Henry VIII & Anne Boleyn) 14, 15, 22
Empson, Richard 5
executions 14, 16, 17, 19, 23

Field of the Cloth of Gold, The 6, 7, 23
Fisher, John 16
Fountains Abbey 12
France and the French 6, 7, 11, 20, 21, 23
Francis I of France 6

Hampton Court 2, 10, 15
hawking 4, 5
Henry VII 3, 4
Hever Castle 2, 10
Holbein, Hans 10, 13, 14, 18, 20
Holy Roman Empire 6, 11
hunting 4, 5, 8

Ireland 16, 20
iron 22, 35

James IV 6
James V 20
Jane Seymour 14, 15, 23
jousting 4, 5

Lancaster 3
London 8
Lord Chancellors 7, 10, 23
Lord Steward 8
Luther, Martin 12

Margaret Tudor (Henry's sister) 6
marriages 5, 11, 14, 18, 19, 23
Mary Rose 2, 20, 21
Mary Stuart, Queen of Scots 20
Mary Tudor 4, 10, 14, 15, 22
monasteries 17, 23
  Dissolution of the 12
money 8
More, Thomas 4, 10, 13, 16
music 4, 9

navy 21
Nonsuch Palace 19

Offaly, Lord 16
Ormondes Castle 2
palaces 8
  see also Hampton Court, Nonsuch
Parliament and laws 8, 12, 13, 14, 22, 23
peace with France 7
Pilgrimage of Grace 17, 23
Pope, the 5, 10, 11, 13, 16, 17, 23

priests 12, 13
Privy Chamber 8, 9

riots and rebellions 17
Rievaulx Abbey 2
Rome 11, 12, 13

Scotland and the Scots 6, 20, 23
servants 8, 9
Spain and the Spanish 3, 5, 6, 8
sport 4

taxes 8, 12, 13, 17, 23
Therouanne 6
Tintern Abbey 2
tithes 12, 23
Tournai 6, 7
Tower of London 2, 7, 16

Union of England and Wales 15

Wales 15, 23
wars 6, 7, 8, 20, 23
Windsor Castle 17
Wolsey, Thomas 7, 10, 11, 23
Wyatt, Sir Thomas 11

Yarmouth Castle 2
York 3